somabasics
water features

soma basics
water features

David Stevens

SOMA

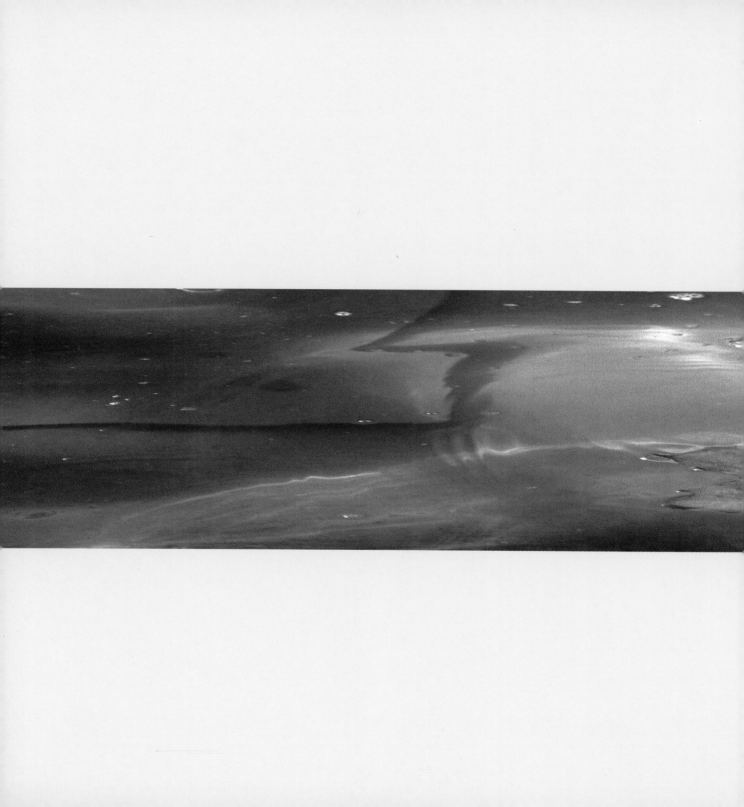

contents

introduction	6	fish & wildlife	86
planning & design	10	address book	92
materials & methods	54	index	94
planting	78	acknowledgments	96

introduction

Opposite *Water can rush or glide, offering the potential for both sound and movement that can transform an ordinary space into a dynamic composition. As the single most important life-sustaining element, it is no wonder that it holds endless fascination.*

The power of water in your garden

Water is both simple and complex. A giver of life and the key to growth, it covers most of our planet's surface. It shapes continents and drives weather systems. It has been harnessed, channeled and used for our service and our pleasure. Water is inexorably woven into the history of gardens. It has appeared everywhere, from the gardens of ancient Egypt and Mesopotamia to the most avant-garde compositions of today.

Water features bring movement, sound, and peace to a garden. They offer habitats for plants, fish and wildlife, but perhaps above all else, they allow us to control and enjoy the most primeval of elements. Like gardens themselves, water features offer endless opportunities. The only limits are those of our own imaginations. As with gardens, it is all too easy to fall into the trap of overcomplication when designing with water. In both cases, the result is a visual disaster.

In this book I have set out to demystify the use of water in the garden and to show how it can be blended into the whole design. Being a designer, I understand the importance of looking at the garden, house and surrounding

environment as a whole. I am aware of the necessity to create a composition that suits you and your family, and I am conscious that the best gardens are essentially simple, always serving you and never the dogma of fashion.

Whether you have a fondness for formal, traditional fountains, for tumbling streams, or for polished granite spheres floating on low-pressure water jets, this book will guide you through choosing and installing your water feature.

It has never been easier to use water as a design element in your garden. The old, complicated methods of constructing features from concrete and other cumbersome materials have largely been superseded, and with them, much of the expense and maintenance traditionally associated with water features. So there really is no excuse for doing without water—the most exciting element in garden design.

Left *By crossing or dividing water you will find yourself manipulating its very nature.*
Above *The manner in which these simple, horizontal pipes contrast with the vertical lines of the planting creates a wonderful effect.*
Opposite *Moving water has a life of its own. Its ever changing patterns dance and swirl in the sunlight.*

planning

& design

Water features are wonderful additions to any garden, but there is no point in rushing into things. Digging a haphazard hole or buying a prefabricated pool will get you nowhere if you haven't thought carefully about what you want, where you want it, and how it will blend into the overall design of the garden.

Opposite *A well-planned water feature takes into account the style of the surrounding garden and environment. Here rich planting links the wider garden seamlessly with the pool edges and continues into the pool itself.*

first steps

Water is a natural element and an essential part of the landscape. To tame it, bringing it within the confines of the garden, takes sensitivity and skill. Because water gardening is a growth industry, more and more speciality supply stores, with a huge range of products and equipment, are opening their doors. For you as a consumer, the danger here is impulse buying, since it can result in a feature that is totally at odds with your garden. More often than not, it will be a pseudonatural watercourse with plastic cascades that drop into a poorly constructed pool surrounded by crazy paving. While I am far from a gardening snob, I honestly feel that such an approach demeans the potential of water and your enjoyment of it.

In most situations one must choose between a natural effect or an artificial feature that is purposefully sculptural or architectural. Both approaches are entirely valid and both rely for their success on blending in with the surrounding composition rather than conflicting with it. This means that the water feature should be planned when you are designing the garden and not simply tacked on as an afterthought.

Inspiration can come from many places including books, garden shows, television programs or magazines. If you take time in planning your garden, you can gather visual images together to create a "mood board." This will help you to rationalize your ideas. In all probability, your garden will be either formal or informal, and the features within the composition will follow suit. Once you have a sense of the style you want, you can start making some positive decisions about your water features.

In many ways formal features are relatively easy to plan, because they link decisively with the geometry that surrounds them. Informal features require additional skills as they must look as though they are natural. In my experience, it is almost impossible to create a natural appearance by looking at pictures, the simple reason being that you have to "feel" water in order to understand its character. The best thing to do is to get out into the country to see how nature does it. Upland areas have enormous character. Take a camera and record how the rock is laid down in strata, how valleys interlock with one another with a stream running through the bottom and how water cascades over it all. Take photographs of falls; see how the rock is undercut, and notice how the stream splits, tumbles and re-forms. Look at pools, rills, boulders and slides, and see how trees and plants grow in naturally formed crevices. In other words, get into it all. The water feature you are trying to create should not be just stuck in the middle of a garden, surrounded by assorted lumps of concrete and sad, sparse shrubs. Water is exciting and dynamic, so make the most of it and enjoy!

Having said all that, the more complex water features are, the more expense is involved. Unfortunately, it is easy to underestimate the cost of creating a garden. In basic terms it will be the "hard landscape" that will take the lion's share of any budget. This will include paving, walling and any major construction work. Rock and terracing, pumps and equipment are not cheap, but if well chosen and correctly constructed they should last a lifetime. Pumps have been improved enormously over the past few years and rarely fail. In addition, they cost virtually nothing to run, so although the initial cost of the investment may seem steep, it is a worthwhile expense. Of course, one advantage of preparing a design for the whole garden is that you can carry out the work in stages, as and when energy, time and funds allow. In other words, as long as space is allocated for a water feature it could easily be phased in as part of a longer-term development plan.

The positioning of any water feature is vitally important and should be carefully considered during the initial planning process. An open area, away from overhanging trees, would be ideal. Ultimate success, however, depends not just on the positioning of a feature, but on a variety of factors, including aquatic planting, adequate oxygenation and the attraction of wildlife to the feature, all of which will be discussed later in the book.

Above left For centuries Japanese gardens have influenced Western design. Water often plays a central role in Japanese design, appearing in pools or streams and flowing over carefully positioned rocks.
Left Even the smallest yard has room for water in some form. Here it is blended into the overall composition, surrounded by cascades of planting.
Opposite Understatement is everything in design. This pot floats on a perfect mirror of water, and the low hedge contains the vision.

Water is endlessly fascinating. There is a place for it in any garden, but the real trick is to integrate it successfully. If your garden is on a slope this is an obvious advantage. Changes in level could be handled either formally or informally, with water dropping down from one level to another. Perhaps you have a fine view with an open area in front of it. A site like this has wonderful potential to house a calm, reflective pool. The water could reflect both the view and the moods of an ever-changing sky. A simple, but no less effective, option is offered by the wall of a tiny yard, where spouts, masks or bowls could transform an otherwise dull situation into a sonorous and entertaining area.

Above *There is always tension between static planting and moving water. In this instance the tension has been heightened by the subtle artifice of the frog. Humor is another factor that can draw the eye and provide a focal point.*
Opposite *A contemporary water feature complements a modern building. Here the pools step down to the lowest curving shape, a form that takes its line from the house itself.*

Above *A sharp contrast in style can be both surprising and dramatic. The crisp white walls of the house set up a wonderful dialogue with the free-form pool and dark rocks. A single tree adds vertical emphasis while the dark water provides a visual link with the rocks.*

Below *If you are going to control water then do it properly and don't take prisoners. The precision of this feature is sheer poetry, the dark, crisp paving containing the rill and defining the steps.*

Above *Contemporary gardens should be just that, with strong lines and a real sense of purpose. The flowing curve of this raised pool makes a definite link with the building. The use of common materials makes a bond between deck and pool, and there is also a connection with the river view.*

choosing a style

Every garden should have a general theme or style, and the water feature should be part of its design. Whatever style you choose, if water is to be part of the garden it must fit into the overall composition. For example, it would be wrong to slap an informal pool down in the middle of a crisp, formal terrace.

In most gardens the house provides the starting point for a design, often suggesting a style. For example, a traditional building with a symmetrical façade may well have a formal garden to match. Following the natural progression of garden spaces the design should become less architectural as it extends from the house. Any garden elements, including water, should follow this progression. Rectangular, interlocking pools near the building could give way to free-form streams, cascades and ponds at the furthest point from the house.

No style should be a straitjacket. At the end of the day, it's your garden, and you must consider your needs and decide what makes you feel comfortable. Remember, fashion has wasted more good money than anything else.

Right *Style is a creative blend of personality and architectural elements. There is enormous tension here between the tiled rectangles, barely touching each another, and the echoing shapes of the hedge. Water provides a link, tying the composition together and adding subtle reflections.*

formal

The word *formality* suggests a regular pattern, a feeling of control, geometry and tradition. In fact, a formal garden can also be quite the opposite, ultramodern and built with high-tech materials. Whatever the period, the formal garden relies on a balanced composition that is symmetrical from side to side or from end to end.

Water is delightful in a formal design. It can be organized into pools set within a terrace or flanking a path; water can also act as a division between different parts of the garden. It might be used as a rill, in a water staircase or simply as a dramatic reflecting pool at the end of a vista.

Above *Formal designs often look their best under minimalist conditions. In this rhythmic pattern, blocks of low hedge are tied together by long pools, punctuated by the reflective balls.*
Right *The permanence of statuary and the transience of a fountain set up a fascinating dialogue. A background hedge marks the boundary of this particular garden "room."*
Opposite *The contrast between youth and age is enhanced by the centrally placed bowl and pool. The background wall provides the canvas for the three-dimensional composition.*

asymmetrical

Asymmetrical design was born out of the modernist movement. It was a reaction against formality, which was seen as a rigid and dated style. Asymmetrical designs still rely on geometry, but instead of the pattern being mirrored, balance is achieved by shapes or features of different visual weights coming into equilibrium by careful positioning within the overall design. For example, a terrace might be built up from a series of overlapping rectangles of paving, planting and water. These rectangles would reflect an underlying grid that picks up on the geometry of the adjoining building. Water could be set at ground level or raised, with an upper pool cascading onto the lower level.

Above Hard and soft elements are positioned in perfect harmony, the crisp reflections of the water providing the ideal link between the two.
Left A zigzagging path through a garden, in this case over water, increases the feeling of space. The slatted stepping decks are at right angles to one another and echo the background screen.
Below Wooden decks always harmonize well with water, both being natural elements. There is an additional visual link here between the angled pools and the timberwork.

In a larger setting, a substantial water feature could be positioned some way into the garden. It might work to offset a garden building, arbor or group of trees elsewhere. While asymmetry requires control and sensitivity in planning, it is often an excellent style adjoining modern houses, or those with an irregular outline.

Opposite There is great power in the cobblestone divide between the upper and lower pools. The raised water is also irresistibly tactile, being within such easy dabbling height.

informal

In many ways this is the most difficult style of all and it is certainly the most abused. The success of an informal garden depends on the designer's ability to understand the workings and shapes of nature, whether a gently meandering river or a bubbling upland stream. The overused kidney-shaped pool is rarely found in the natural environment.

Sensitivity is all in an informal situation. For example, you might have virtually the whole of a garden given over to a naturalistic pool lushly planted with indigenous species, perhaps with a beautifully detailed deck for a dash of control. Alternatively, your garden might move from the architectural to the informal in a smooth transition of space. Both approaches are quite valid.

Right *An informal style can be created with flowing lines, soft planting, smooth boulders or cascading waterfalls. The secret is to produce an unconscious simulation of the landscape, using natural materials and subtle effects. This waterfall is perfectly constructed; the rocks are all laid on a precisely horizontal bedding plane. The sound of running water will be particularly beautiful on a summer day.*

Opposite left *A well-worn piece of timber acts as a channel for a small stream of water that drops into a rocky pool, demonstrating that found materials can be just as effective as store-bought ones.*

Opposite right *A large boulder, drilled through its middle, makes an effective centerpiece. The rock is securely supported under the water.*

Opposite below *The crisp lines of a white wall strike a note of formality in an otherwise informal composition. The horizontal line of the wall is cleverly set off by vertical planting.*

ways with water

Although the variety of ways in which water can be used are limitless, we have already seen that any feature should be chosen or adapted to suit the overall garden style. Water is a rich habitat, and your feature could support a whole range of plants, fish and other wildlife. Most ponds and pools are suitable for fish, and a larger pool might also be a haven for wildfowl. Fish can live in streams and rills, but these features are more likely to suit planting. In a pool the planting could be lush and informal, while in a rill it might be unashamedly architectural.

Bog gardens are a plantsman's paradise. No irrigation is needed here and the plants produce dynamic foliage that lasts all summer long. On a smaller scale, a simple cobble and boulder feature can be fascinating and also safe for young children. Or why not go really high-tech and build a "water port" like the one opposite? (See also page 50.) Remember that the ideas that follow are intended to act as catalysts: the only limit to what you can achieve is your imagination.

Right *The effects that you can achieve with water are endless. They can be subtle, straightforward or downright humorous. The secret of success lies not just in imagination but also in the construction. The feature must function perfectly, but the mechanics of it must remain invisible. The end result may be bold or deliciously delicate, as here, with the humor shining through.*

Above *In my own gardens I take the dynamics of water to their limits, playing endlessly with color, movement, planting and anything else that will take the art form forward. This spectacular water slide is divided into alternate chutes of water and plants. It runs out from the house, over a sitting area and driveway, across a pool and into the bed on the far side. The construction of all this had to be worked out from scratch, the pumps and piping concealed and the whole thing made watertight to protect the people sitting beneath. It worked beautifully.*

pools & ponds

As we have seen, the style of your water feature can vary from the strictly formal to the completely naturalistic, and pools and ponds are no exception. Whatever style you choose, your pool or pond will probably be a large and relatively open area of water. In purely practical terms, the larger the pool, the easier it will be to maintain. This is because its size will allow the ideal balance of plants, fish and other aquatic life. Pests, such as mosquitoes, can be controlled by the helpful inmates of your pool. It is difficult to achieve this healthy balance in pools less than 6½ feet square, so try to make them at least this big, and larger if you possibly can.

If we think of the garden as a natural extension of the house, it makes sense to start by planning the pools that will be closest to the house. The link between inside and out should be a strong one and, in the right circumstances, water could actually be made to extend from an interior room to an outside one, separated only by a sheet of glass dipping just below the surface. Fish and plants can live in either environment. In the case of a swimming pool, people could even swim from house to garden!

The dimensions of any pool close to the house should ideally conform to your overall paving design, fitting comfortably into the pattern rather than breaking across it. In other words, if you lifted out a number of slabs, an area of deck or some sections of an overall design grid that is based on the proportions of the house, the pool would fit neatly into it.

Right Ponds and pools can be as large or as small as you like. This is a perfect study in the art of the miniature, and it brings great intimacy to this corner of the garden. The pattern on the bowl is a subtle touch, as it echoes the form of the lily.

Opposite By paying attention to detail and using local materials you are bound to create a worthwhile composition. Although this is essentially a formal design, the cobblestones soften the outline, blending it into the path in the foreground. The slight change in level makes the rill drip into the lower pool, providing both sound and movement.

Right *The character of a pool can be greatly influenced by plants. In this pool plants are the defining element, practically covering the whole surface. Such an approach both softens the surrounding paving and incorporates the water feature into the wider garden.*

If we think of the garden as a natural extension of the house, it makes sense to start by planning the pools around the building.

The simplest pool should be set just below the terrace surface with the surrounding paving acting as a precise coping. Rather more complex designs can incorporate split-level pools. The higher level might be set at 18 inches and made wider so that it could double as an occasional seat. The water would flow over a sill into the lower pool. In this case, the lower pool should be considerably larger than the upper one; otherwise it would overflow when the circulating pump is switched off. Such a composition could also include split-level planting, built-in seating or even a barbecue.

As one moves farther away from the house, the shapes of the water features can become progressively less formal, echoing those of the surrounding design. The pool might be surrounded by paving, or it might be a more naturalistic type of pond, bounded by grass, planting or a full-blown bog garden. There could be a deck, sitting area or arbor, but whatever the composition, a pool positioned at some distance from the house will become a major focal point.

Remember that the view to or from such a feature really is an important consideration—there's no point in gazing fondly at the back of your garage or its reflection in the water (unless it is incredibly attractive!)—so make sure that you think about this when deciding where to position your pool.

Left *Reflections play endlessly with light. They can dance with a breeze or mirror the view on a still day. The essence of this design is in its subtle movement, from the stone bubble fountain in the foreground, and the rill with its strong directional emphasis, to the calm sheet of water framed by paving and a low hedge. The overall feeling is one of control, and this sits comfortably with the symmetrical façade of the house.*

streams, rills & canals

All three of these features suggest both visual and physical movement. They lead the eye in a given direction and form a physical link between separate areas of water. Again, we have a division between the formal geometry of rills and canals and the informality of streams.

Historic houses and gardens are often richly formal. There are wonderful lessons to be learned by visiting them, armed with a camera and notebook. Sir Edwin Lutyens, the great English architect and garden designer, was a master of geometry. He used superbly detailed rills, pools and canals to create subtle links between house and garden. Rills are narrow, often only 12 inches or so across, and this visually compresses the water to create a real feeling of tension as the feature runs from one larger area of water to another. For a rill to be really effective it needs to be as long as reasonably possible. In a large garden the length might be several hundred yards. Rills normally contain little planting since the space is so limited. However, small reeds and rushes can add a delicate vertical emphasis against a long horizontal line.

Canals are also long and comparatively narrow, but on a larger scale, often moving large amounts of water, such as from one pond to another. They firmly belong to the formal school, whether this be traditional or modern. When positioned with sensitivity they have an enormous potential to draw the eye and provide stunning reflections. In my opinion they are best planted with low-growing aquatics, such as lilies. Fountains detract from the canal's ability to mirror the sky or neighboring features.

Right *Controlling an essentially powerful element, while preserving its inherent mystery, is essential in the design of rills and canals. Here a formal structure combined with the dark surface achieves this balance.*
Opposite *Water is astonishing in its power, seeming to slash its way through the surrounding paving.*

The real secret of success is to create something that looks natural.

Below *Streams are alive with movement, and in a garden this can take many different forms. This white cobblestone beach would rarely be found in nature, but in a controlled setting it brings reflected light and a sharp contrast to the immediate surroundings.*

Above *Architectural and natural features are juxtaposed here, each enhancing the other, while the strong lines of the foreground provide a focus for the rocks.*

Streams are full of movement and they need a slope, natural or artificial, to work well. Once again, scale is everything, and as a general rule the more generous the feature the better. A stream's character can be upland or lowland, the former with rock and flying water, the latter much calmer, with reduced flow rates and lusher planting. The gradient of your garden will tell you which is the most appropriate choice.

When creating artificial slopes, great care should be taken to make them look convincing. The real secret of success is to create something that looks natural. This is another reason for getting to know the environment. Streams ebb and flow. They have pools that are deep and rapids that are shallow. They are undercut on the outside of bends and they deposit silt on the inside. If you are a kid at heart, as I am, there is nothing better than playing around on the river or stream, so go for it!

Above *Water can so easily tease you from one section of the garden to the next; here the stream gives way to a rill, which in turn feeds the pool. Pyramids of foliage guard the space, providing a frame of vertical lines above the reflective floor.*

fountains

Fountains are the exclamation points of a garden, demanding as much, if not more, attention than any other major focal point. They can range from the simplest jet that just breaks the surface with a bubble, to grand affairs that soar many feet into the air.

The simplest fountain is a single plume. In addition to its visual value, it can help to aerate a pool, benefiting fish during hot weather. The height or volume of the jet will relate to the size of the pool. If a tall plume is installed in a small pond the slightest breeze will quickly empty the feature. A small bubble jet is the perfect addition to an intimate sitting area.

On a practical level, the most common method of driving a fountain is the submersible pump. Many have adjustable valves to raise or lower the flow. If installed correctly they are perfectly safe and will run for many years at minimal expense. In between these two extremes are all kinds of variations, some of which can be astonishingly beautiful, but some of which, unfortunately, can be mere ill-conceived gimmicks. As with most other elements in the garden, it is generally the simple designs that look the best.

You have only to visit some of the great Renaissance gardens in Italy to see that there are no limits to the possibilities of water. Equally stunning features are

Left *Fountains are the dancers in the world of water. Classical or contemporary, they add vibrancy and movement. There is great rhythm here, not just in the relationship of these acrylic tubes but in the bubbles that rise and swirl through them.*
Opposite *Any radius needs a pivot. In this case it is provided by a simple plume rising from the circular, cobblestone-filled pool. The curving background wall holds the design together; it is a perfect backdrop for the cascade of foliage, which drapes downward, and the fountain, which shoots upward.*

being created for gardens today on a smaller and more domestic scale. A great friend of mine designs "flat" fountains made from sheets of stainless steel in various sizes. Slots are cut in the sheets so that water spills in ripples and rills over the polished surface. The effect is magical.

"Floating balls" are one of my favorite forms of fountain. They are made from perfectly formed stone spheres that measure up to 6½ feet across. The sphere is set in a matching stone container, where it "floats" on low-pressure jets of water, turning slowly this way and that, catching the sun and the imagination in a continuous pattern of reflective movement.

Below *There is something wonderfully mysterious about water welling up and over the sides of this dark bowl, the whole arrangement set about with flower and foliage.*

Above *Pyramids have a unique primeval and visual force that dates back to the Egyptians. Water is a natural accompaniment. The stepped sides of this structure evoke a chiseled rock face. Rills add control in this situation, tying the feature into the wider garden.*

Above *This is a wonderful example of an organic water feature. It echoes the shape of tropical urchin shells. Groups of three always look comfortable, and the whole arrangement is perfectly set off by the pale gravel that covers the reservoir and mechanics beneath. Low planting and grasses are the perfect foil, the tufted shapes enhancing rather than fighting against the rounded domes.*

wall-mounted features

Many gardens are too small for a pool, but space limitations need not prevent you from bringing water into your design. In town gardens the wall area is often considerably greater than that of the floor, but it is frequently ignored or underused. Once we start to consider the potential of the vertical planes of the garden we start to realize that walls can support all kinds of planting, in baskets or boxes, in built-in furniture and, of course, in water.

By now it will be clear that the choice of feature should be defined by the period of the building and the style of the garden. The problem is that most garden centers stock a preponderance of so-called "classical" items—cherubs relieving themselves or lions endlessly regurgitating water. Don't buy the first thing you see; shop around and think of the style you wish to enhance. While there is nothing wrong with a classical item in a formal garden, an increasing number of designers are offering abstract or just good contemporary wall-mounted features. The best places to hunt these out are garden shows, where you will find an enormous range of innovative work.

Water has a strong power of attraction—it draws the eye. Remember this when choosing a position for your water feature. All too often a mask or bowl is placed

Remember those vital design ingredients: tension, mystery and surprise.

Right *With a wall-mounted feature the spout is as much an attraction as the water itself. These can be classical or contemporary—here there is a real contrast between the mythical fish and the dry stone wall behind. This is an important point: the background should always be low-key, allowing the feature to shine through.*

Right *In an intimate space you can place a feature close to eye level. Water can change direction and these copper stems and cups seem to mimic calla lilies, themselves lovers of water. Copper is not only easy to shape but over time it acquires a wonderful patina.*

Above While the classical pouting and spouting mask is ever popular, it can be worked in a thousand different ways. Tufa rock suggests a grotto, water cascading into a damp green fernery below.
Opposite Taps are water workhorses, but with a little imagination they can be transformed into decorative elements.

directly opposite a door or window. By drawing the eye, it has the effect of foreshortening the space. In terms of overall design, it may be better to think of a position just out of immediate view. The enticing sound of the water positioned out of sight, but just within earshot, will draw you into another part of the garden, increasing the feeling of space. Remember those vital design ingredients: tension, mystery and surprise. These elements allow a garden to unfold in a series of different moods and "rooms."

If you are creative and competent, why not design and install your own water feature? It could be a series of polished copper cups, set vertically, with one overflowing into another and pouring into a bowl at the lowest level. One or more upright acrylic tubes of different heights could have water welling up within and over them, economical on space and wonderful when lit from below at night. Alternatively, in a garden with a classical theme, you might find a stone mask and use it to create a striking feature. It would be easy enough to drill through the mask and attach a pipe and spout. Designing your own feature enables you to put part of your personality into your garden and create something that is completely in tune with its mood.

The construction of all of these features, which I shall look at in greater detail later on, is quite straight-forward, requiring a small reservoir, submersible pump and simple piping. They are also low maintenance—all that is needed is for the water to be topped off to compensate for evaporation.

The enticing sound of water positioned out of sight, but just within earshot, will draw you into another part of the garden, increasing the feeling of space.

small-scale features

Of all water features, these can be the most innovative and they are certainly my own favorites. They not only fit into the smallest of areas but can also be made from a vast range of different materials.

The whole trend started off with the simple millstone fountain: enormous and durable, millstones create impressive features. The hole in the middle of the millstone is positioned over a water tank. A submersible pump is positioned at the bottom and connected to a pipe that runs up through the stone, stopping just below the top surface. When the pump is switched on, water flows up and over the surface, then returns to the tank in a continuous cycle. The whole feature is often surrounded by loose stones, together with planting.

The whole trend started off with the simple millstone fountain: enormous and durable, millstones create impressive features.

Today you can buy imitation millstones. While some of these almost look the part, many of them are decidedly false, being poorly constructed from fiberglass. The real mark of a millstone is its size. Most real ones measure at least a yard across, while artificial versions are a half or a third of that and look puny and feeble as a result.

Many years ago we started experimenting with a whole range of other materials, using the same principle of a pump, reservoir and connecting pipe to create all kinds of different effects. I remember that the first was an old slate pier head, approximately 2 feet square, with gently sloping sides. When a hole was drilled through the middle, water slid over the polished surface and

Above *Isn't this just drop-dead gorgeous? I saw this copper leaf at a flower show some years ago and I have wanted to use it ever since! There is supreme subtlety and craftsmanship here, with water being gently pumped up and over the surface. The secret is to blend it into a leafy background, so that you have to look twice to appreciate what is really going on.*

Right *This is a pure study in the relationships of different forms and textures, the glistening water boulder contrasting with the ribbed hosta leaves in the background. Ferns provide yet another foreground shape, reveling in the damp conditions.*

Opposite *When constructed properly and positioned with sensitivity, this kind of feature is hard to beat in a confined space. Simplicity is often the key. In this type of arrangement water should flow gently rather than gush. When using bowls or containers, do check that they are frostproof, since the combination of water and freezing conditions can be deadly.*

looked wonderful. Exactly the same technique can be used for a fine glazed or terra-cotta bowl standing in a bed of stones. The feed pipe is sealed through the base of the bowl, which is filled with water. The pump is activated and water gushes, or wells, depending on how you control the flow, over the edges and back into the reservoir. Try laying the bowl down—or use two bowls, or three, of different diameters or heights—the permutations are endless.

Smooth or rough boulders can be drilled and used in the same way. I recently designed the most beautiful stainless-steel water boulder, a highly polished hemisphere set in a bed of ruby-red glass beads that sparkle in the sun. But perhaps the greatest advantage of all these features is their safety. Provided construction is carried out correctly and the water reservoir is quite secure, there are no areas of open water that might be a danger to toddlers. I do of course exclude an open bowl from this category. Common sense must be applied when choosing your water feature.

Above *You don't need a torrent to create a focal point, just a small change of level to stir the imagination. The secret here is to adjust the flow and the angle of the slide so that water drops cleanly into the pool below. The warped timber slats offer a delightful feeling of informality, but they may need replacing on a regular basis if rot sets in.*

structural features

This is where the big-time imagination comes into play, and why not! Most of us are far too conservative when it comes to introducing water into our gardens. There are any number of ways to employ it on a large scale and the effects are wonderful.

Everybody knows about carports, but few people have a "water port." We built the one shown on page 29 from a sloping structure of steel and clear acrylic, angled down from the house toward a pool. Water is pumped to the top and slides down the acrylic, creating a spectacular combination of sound, reflection and movement. Water arbors can be constructed in much the same way, with catchment pools to either side of the arbor; a similar treatment could be used for a water arch. High-level planting can be incorporated into any of these structures, being housed within troughs that have irrigation built in.

Water walls are also spectacular and can be constructed from any number of materials. Usually a trough along the top overflows and spills water down the wall into a long pond below. Water stairs are yet another variation on the theme of falling water. They work with a submersible pump circulating water from bottom to top. The effect of the water gliding over and down the stairs is magical, particularly when lit by dancing beams of sunlight.

Right *"Structural" means just that—it implies a feeling of permanence and stability. Such features often provide dynamic focal points, leading the eye positively across or through the garden and terminating the view with a definite full stop. Here the raised rill beckons you toward the white picture-frame walls, where a canvas of water is punctuated by a fountain jet. There is great perspective here, which is sharpened by the austerity of simple foliage set against the walls.*

Right *This is a contemporary Mediterranean garden that I built to reflect the harshness of the local landscape and then softened it with water. A major feature was the water curtain, made from rusting scaffolding tube to reflect the color of the surrounding landscape. Water drops gently but steadily along the length of the feature, setting up ripples that bring the pool to life with sound and movement.*

bog gardens

I've left the best to last. To have a bog garden is to have plants—and what plants! The real joy about such an area is the simple fact that you never have to water it and everything grows like mad. Of course, you have to choose the right species for the site, but many of these are really spectacular, from the huge leaves of *Gunnera manicata*, fantastic in a large garden but definitely not for the fainthearted, to the delicacy of any of the bog primroses that are more suitable for a smaller garden. There are hundreds of others, and real favorites include hostas, ligularias, rodgersia and iris.

In visual and practical terms, a boggy area naturally adjoins a stream or pool and is rarely found as an isolated feature. It will need to be linked with the main area of water so that moisture can seep in. A bog garden is a damp area but it needs drainage or it will stagnate and be unable to support plant life.

Above Foliage is the crowning glory of a bog garden and huge plants like Gunnera manicata can absorb all the moisture they need from the damp ground. The maintenance of such planting combinations is really limited to thinning out when necessary.

Right above and below *Foliage can be dramatic and so can flowers, particularly when they are used in great sweeps and drifts of color as though someone had just cast bucketfuls of bloom over the garden. These bog primroses are particularly attractive when combined with species like cardinal flower, iris and purple loosestrife.*

materials

& methods

The best water features look either completely natural or crisply architectural, and the secret of both is impeccable construction. While most techniques are straightforward, they need to be fully understood, which in turn asks for a degree of practicality and a knowledge of the materials involved. In this section I will take you through all of the techniques, letting you in on a few trade secrets on the way.

using liners

Over the past twenty years pool liners have revolutionized construction of water features. The easy availability of durable, relatively low-cost liners that are quick and easy to install has made it possible for anyone with basic skills and knowledge to build a simple water feature in their own garden. Additionally, liners are extremely adaptable, lending themselves to the construction of various styles of feature, from pools and waterfalls to streams and rills. Liners are sheets of plastic or, more durable still, tough butyl rubber, which can be bought in different grades or thicknesses. Most good garden centers sell liners in standard sizes. If you

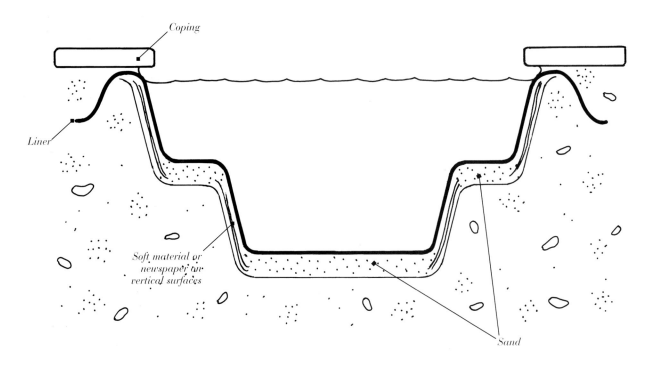

Coping

Liner

Soft material or newspaper on vertical surfaces

Sand

Above and opposite *Although flexible liners are invaluable in pools and water features, they need to be concealed completely with coping if they are to be visually effective. They are sturdy, but care needs to be taken in construction. Sharp stones should be removed and the sheet should be bedded on a layer of sand. Smooth out the liner and run water into the pool to mold it to the excavation. Trim any excess liner away and lay paving, or another material, to overhang the edges.*

are building a pool to a nonstandard size, you can follow this simple formula to estimate the size of the sheet you'll need: add twice the depth to both the maximum length and width of the proposed pool or feature. If you are contemplating the construction of a water feature covering a very large area, you can get sections of liner welded together to your specifications. This technique can also be used for smaller, rectangular pools, where liners can be welded into a box shape so that they fit exactly into the area allocated for them, doing away with

Right and below *Beaches provide an attractive visual transition between water and dry land. They also conceal the liner and allow wildlife, such as frogs and small mammals, easy access to the water. The liner is bedded on 4 inches of sand and covered with either soil, which allows aquatic plants to root easily, or mortar, which offers physical protection. Materials used to construct the beach should be compatible with the overall composition. Don't make the beach too regular since this will look artificial. Mix up the stones to create a more natural effect.*

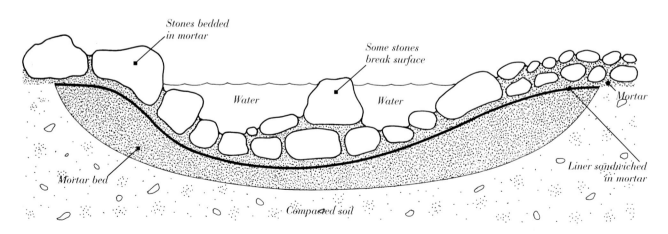

Stones bedded in mortar

Some stones break surface

Water

Water

Mortar

Mortar bed

Liner sandwiched in mortar

Compacted soil

Right and below *The secret to building an effective informal waterfall system is concealment of the liner, to make the feature look as natural as possible. The liner is laid over sand on horizontal surfaces and behind the vertical walls that separate the various levels. These walls should be built with solid concrete foundations in order to help stabilize the whole feature. The principles of construction of informal waterfall systems are similar to those of formal systems—the difference lies in the materials chosen.*

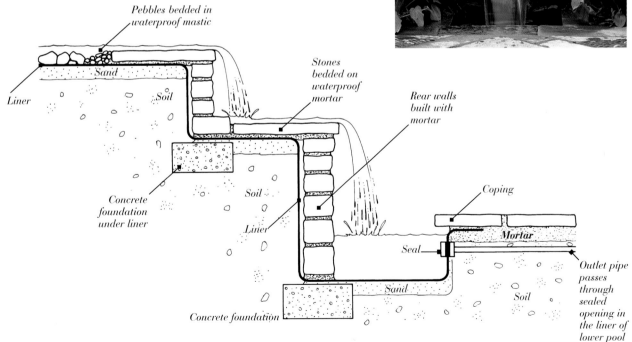

Pebbles bedded in waterproof mastic

Sand

Liner

Soil

Stones bedded on waterproof mortar

Rear walls built with mortar

Concrete foundation under liner

Soil

Liner

Coping

Seal

Mortar

Concrete foundation

Sand

Soil

Outlet pipe passes through sealed opening in the liner of lower pool

preformed pools

the need for complicated tucks and folds at the corners. Black liners are the best choice for most applications since they are virtually invisible when covered with water. Avoid patterned or colored liners, particularly blue ones and those with simulated pebbles—they look awful.

Concealment of the liner is an important consideration when designing a water feature. There is nothing worse than seeing a strip of wrinkled plastic or rubber lying around the top of a pool. Provided the pool rim is absolutely level and the surrounding coping overhangs the water by about 1½ inches, then the resulting shadow should disguise the small amount of liner showing. Alternatively, if the outer skin of the pool is built from bricks or blocks, the liner can be inserted partway through it and sandwiched in the middle of the wall.

The liner for a stream can be laid over a smooth concrete base and covered with wet mortar. It can be completely concealed by stones tipped onto the stream bed when the mortar is still wet. This is where your imagination comes in. Make the feature as natural as possible, using larger stones to create pools and divisions within the stream.

Whether they are formal or informal in design, waterfalls need careful construction to make them fully watertight. Any leakage of water can eventually cause damage to the pump if the circulating system runs dry. An excellent tip is to have liners of ample size. If you need to use more than one sheet, overlap the top over the bottom so that the water flows smoothly off one and on to the next.

These are the easiest pools to install as they can be bought ready to use in a wide variety of shapes and sizes. The smaller pools are less useful because they cannot maintain the correct balance of plants, fish and other aquatic life. Free-form shapes are often too convoluted for use in an architectural design, but they may fit into the less formal parts of the garden, particularly if the pool's edges are completely concealed by coping or planting.

Pools are usually constructed from molded plastic or black fiberglass, in various shapes and sizes. Shallow shelves for aquatic species planted in baskets are often incorporated around the edges, 10 inches below the water line, but the common depth of approximately 18 inches is not deep enough for large fish, such as koi carp, which need far more spacious conditions in which to live.

Opposite above and below *Preformed pools are relatively quick and easy to install. The outline of the pool should be marked out and dug down to the level of the pool's shelf. Trace the outline of the deepest area and dig out to the finished depth. Bed the pool on sand or sifted soil, then backfill around the edges, compacting the sand or soil carefully to prevent the pool from moving. Bed the surrounding coping rocks securely in mortar. Natural stone coping like this is ideal around a preformed pool as it completely conceals the edges. There is a good balance of pond life here, with lilies and marginal plants offering an excellent environment for fish. Planting outside the pool helps to incorporate it into the wider setting.*

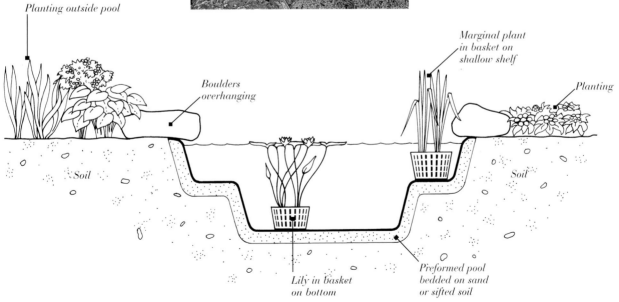

Planting outside pool

Boulders overhanging

Marginal plant in basket on shallow shelf

Planting

Soil

Soil

Lily in basket on bottom

Preformed pool bedded on sand or sifted soil

concrete

Concrete is time consuming to prepare, pour and set. In addition, older ponds can begin to leak on account of subsidence or other external influences. Such leaks are often almost impossible to find, and as a consequence, the features become unusable and need complete rebuilding. There are situations, however, where concrete really is the best material to use. The awkward angles and interconnecting shapes of some pools or linked features would be very difficult to construct with a liner, particularly if there is a fall from one level to another.

The real secret to working in concrete is to use suitable reinforcement and build up the structure in layers. Sound and well-compacted foundations are essential and, in an informal situation, wire mesh or chain-link fence is sandwiched in the middle of the concrete to provide integral strength. With more formal work, a wooden form is used to contain the concrete, with bent steel reinforcing rods tying the bottom and sides together. In order to keep the whole structure waterproof, a suitable additive must be incorporated into the mix. A final coat of a black waterproof paint is generally used to finish the job.

Above right and right This is a simple concrete block pool with a waterproof, rendered finish. It is gloriously uncomplicated and, being low-key, fits perfectly into the overall garden. The bottom of this pool is a single cast-concrete slab. Hollow concrete-block walls are built up over reinforcing rods already set in the bottom section, and the blocks are then filled with more concrete to stabilize the whole structure. A waterproof mastic is then applied and finished with a black sealant.

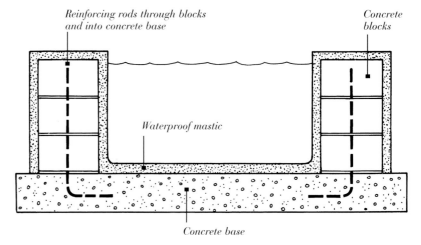

Reinforcing rods through blocks and into concrete base

Concrete blocks

Waterproof mastic

Concrete base

Right and below *This is an elegant and complex feature of a highly architectural nature. Anyone contemplating building such an arrangement would be well advised to employ a specialist landscape contractor. Water bubbles from the bowl, spilling over into the top pool and the rill, which then descends to the lower rill and pool. The rills and pools are made from concrete that was cast in a wooden form in order to achieve very precise measurements. The whole feature is rendered with waterproof mortar and the surrounding paving laid as a neat coping. Reinforcing rods are used throughout the construction to ensure rigidity and prevent cracking. The diamond pattern of the stones complements the paving around the fountain in the foreground.*

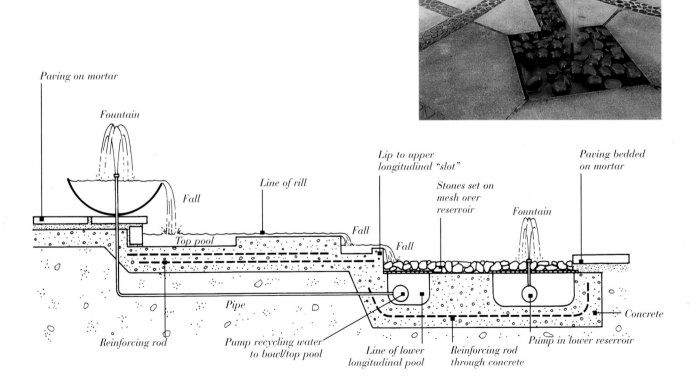

Paving on mortar

Fountain

Lip to upper longitudinal "slot"

Paving bedded on mortar

Line of rill

Stones set on mesh over reservoir

Fountain

Fall

Fall

Fall

Top pool

Pipe

Concrete

Reinforcing rod

Pump recycling water to bowl/top pool

Line of lower longitudinal pool

Reinforcing rod through concrete

Pump in lower reservoir

other materials

I have already whetted your appetite for those small-scale water features that can be so neatly tucked into a corner, bringing focus to a small, intimate area. Although most of them use the "pump and sump" principle, sound construction is essential if they are to work properly. Again, the real secret is to conceal all of the working parts, so that the whole composition looks as natural as possible.

In broad terms, there are two types of these features, those set above ground, in some kind of raised area, and those placed at ground level with the sump, or reservoir, buried out of sight. Relatively small features look most attractive set above ground. This brings the whole arrangement closer to eye level and, if set within a raised bed and given generous coping, it can double as an occasional seat. In my experience, a larger reservoir is always better than a small one. It needs topping off less frequently and there is more room to work. Heavy-duty molded plastic water tanks are ideal and these can be placed within a raised bed and positioned on a layer of sand or sifted soil.

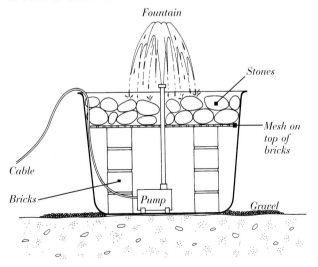

Left and above *This kind of feature is very easy to construct. Ideally, it should be tucked into a corner and surrounded by planting, as it is here, helping it to form a natural part of the composition. It is driven by a small, submersible pump set at the bottom of the bowl. Bricks are built up from the bottom to support a wire mesh, which in turn supports stones of various sizes. Fill with water, switch the pump on and allow the water to dance over the stones. Maintenance includes keeping the surface clear of leaves and debris, as well as topping off during hot weather.*

Left and below *Garden design is an art form. I have a great love of reflective surfaces, particularly when they are associated with water. I created this hemisphere from stainless steel in a straightforward "pump and sump" design, with the water bubbling gently from top to bottom. The whole arrangement rests in a sea of glass beads that sparkle in the sun. Beneath the feature lies a tank, somewhat bigger than the hemisphere, inside which are piers that support both the hemisphere and a fine metal mesh that prevents the beads falling through into the water. Incorporate a removable section of mesh so that you can reach the pump if necessary, and then have fun pouring out those sparkling beads.*

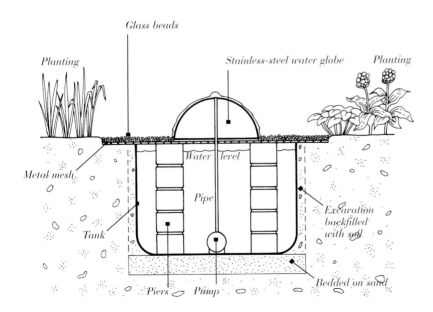

Glass beads

Planting

Stainless-steel water globe

Planting

Water level

Metal mesh

Pipe

Tank

Excavation backfilled with soil

Piers

Pump

Bedded on sand

Make sure the tank is absolutely level and build suitable piers inside it to support your chosen feature, whether it is a large, smooth boulder, a millstone or anything else your imagination comes up with. The piers should reach to just below the top of the tank. A submersible pump at the bottom of the tank provides the power to drive the water contained within the feature. Remember that electricity can be lethal; always seek professional help if in the slightest doubt. If the feature is surrounded by loose stones or pebbles you will need to install some kind of mesh, strong enough to carry the weight involved. Plastic-coated steel mesh can be particularly useful; leave a removable section so that you can reach the pump if necessary. This overall principle of construction can also be used for sunken features. A dipstick is useful for checking the water level.

A smaller feature can be constructed within a glazed bowl or wooden half-barrel. The workings would be exactly the same but a flexible rubber or plastic liner would be needed to keep the barrel watertight. Such arrangements can be delightful when planted with miniature aquatics, a bubble jet just breaking the water's surface.

You will find many kits sold in garden centers that include all the necessary working parts for a complete feature. You can build these in their entirety or buy the components separately, as I have described, to build something unique. Over to you!

Opposite *"Less is more"—the battle cry of the modern movement—is as pertinent today as it was some sixty years ago. There is an austere and beautiful simplicity about this juxtaposition of natural and man-made elements. The contrast between them emphasizes the qualities of both. The wonderful, deep-pink lily stands out against the concrete wall. The wall's subtle pattern adds background texture to the composition.*

bog gardens

Bog gardens are ideal for plant lovers, and there is a huge array of plants that will thrive in such conditions and provide spectacular displays. However, there is more to the art of making a bog garden than simply creating a wet and stagnant area in the middle of your lawn. The secret is to maintain moisture in the earth rather than creating an area of standing water, which would simply suffocate the plants. Bog gardens look best when they adjoin a pool or stream, although they can also be constructed as freestanding features in the garden.

A flexible liner offers the easiest way to create a foundation for the garden. If the bog is an extension of a pool or stream, the liner should be bedded over a smooth concrete strip foundation, just below the water level of the adjoining feature. It should then be sandwiched between stones set in mortar. These stones stabilize the bank and allow water to seep into the boggy area.

The liner should be laid over a layer of gravel, which in turn is placed over sand or sifted soil. Punch 1- to 2-inch slots in the liner approximately 24 inches apart and spread a layer of gravel over the top to ensure adequate drainage. The feature should then be topped off with good-quality top soil, bringing it slightly higher than the surrounding surface, to allow for settlement. The soil should be approximately 12 inches deep.

The method of construction is similar for a freestanding bog garden, but such a feature would obviously need to be kept damp with either an irrigation system or by hand watering.

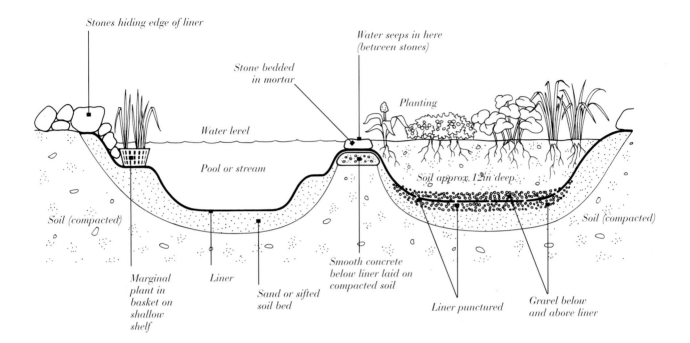

Stones hiding edge of liner

Water seeps in here
(between stones)

Stone bedded
in mortar

Planting

Water level

Pool or stream

Soil approx. 12in deep

Soil (compacted)

Soil (compacted)

Marginal
plant in
basket on
shallow
shelf

Liner

Sand or sifted
soil bed

Smooth concrete
below liner laid on
compacted soil

Liner punctured

Gravel below
and above liner

Opposite and above *Rich, rich planting is the stuff of bog gardens, full of flowers and foliage that thrive in such damp conditions. The edge of this stream gently rises above water level, boasting a wide range of different-colored iris and bog primroses. The success of this scheme lies in the bold use of drifts, rather than individual specimens. The liner that forms the open water has been extended to underlie the bog garden. This has been done in such a way that water can seep between the stones set in mortar. You should incorporate a concrete strip foundation beneath the liner to prevent erosion. In the bog garden area, gravel should be laid both below and above the liner to aid drainage.*

pumps & equipment

The area that has improved above all others in water garden construction is that of pumps and associated fittings. Submersible pumps now come in a huge range of sizes and specifications. Go to a good water garden center and find the right pump for the job. As with everything else in this field, concealment is the name of the game; a pump should be positioned beneath an overhang of rock or in the shadow of a stepping stone. Pipes used to transport water to the top of the feature should also be carefully concealed. The pipes are normally buried, which is quite satisfactory until you forget where they are and puncture them with a garden fork! Accidents can be avoided by marking the position of the pipe with stones so that you always remember where it is.

It is almost inevitable that you will want to adjust the flow to a fountain, waterfall or other arrangement. To that end, it should be simple enough to install a gate valve, usually right next to the pump, in an easily accessible position. Larger above-ground pumps are sometimes used for major projects. However, these are more problematic, require complicated piping, and need to be housed in chambers that are often unsightly. If you are contemplating such a major project, then it is almost certainly best to hire a specialist contractor.

Right and opposite *Although it looks impressive, this kind of feature is easy enough to construct, working on the "pump and sump" principle. The trellis sits on the edge of the copper container, concealing a pipe neatly behind one of the slats. This is connected to the top cup and water spills from one to the next, eventually falling back into the bucket. It is essential that the pump be fitted with a valve so the flow can be delicately adjusted and does not simply gush all over the feature.*

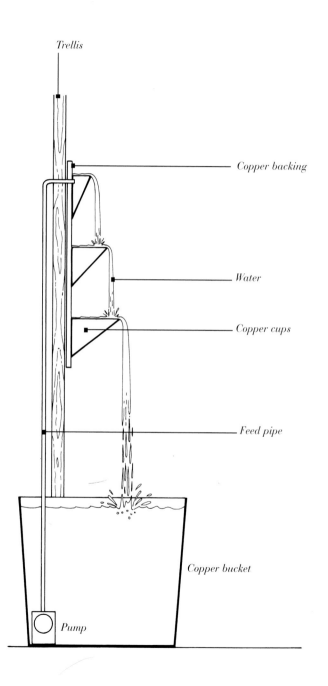

Trellis

Copper backing

Water

Copper cups

Feed pipe

Copper bucket

Pump

electricity

Electricity is the driving force for most water features. It is absolutely essential to use it sensibly and install it correctly. If in doubt enlist the services of a qualified electrician—it is far better to be safe than sorry. Most pumps will run on a grounded 120-volt outlet; for safety reasons, many city electrical codes require the use of GFCI (ground-circuit fault interrupter) outlets. All equipment bought from a reputable garden center will include full installation instructions that should be followed to the letter. If you are running a number of features, pumps or lights it can make sense to install a circuit, with GFCI outlets strategically placed around the garden, providing power to your outdoor electrical features. Installing a circuit is usually a professional job. Cables should be armored and buried at a safe depth so that they cannot be reached by garden tools.

If you are carrying out a complete redesign of the garden, or starting from scratch, it can make good sense to plan the cable runs right at the beginning when it will be easy to dig any necessary trenches and lay the cables. The planned features can always be built and connected at a later date. Never underestimate the number of places that you may need power; aim to be slightly over, rather than under, what you actually need.

lighting

Though you may not often think about it, our gardens and the features contained within them are dark for approximately half the year. While we primarily use the space during daylight, there is enormous scope for evening and nighttime use, which is where lighting comes into its own. Subtlety is everything with garden lighting, "less is more" being a sensible principle. Even simple lights can cast a complexity of shadows.

Water features are always focal points, whatever their size, and it follows that lighting should focus on them, leaving the immediate surroundings to act as a quiet backdrop. Before you think about anything else, consider color for a moment. Forget all the garish hues like yellow, red and orange—they turn foliage unattractive colors. Blue and white light are by far the best to use, enhancing the surroundings rather than detracting from them.

Different lighting techniques produce different effects. The simplest are floodlighting and spotlighting. Spotlights use a hidden source and a tight beam to pinpoint a feature and throw it into sharp relief, while floodlights provide a softer and rather gentler spread of light. Backlighting is just what you might expect: a relatively low light source behind the feature, again throwing it into relief in an altogether more subtle way.

Stunning effects can be obtained by using waterproof lighting set within a pool or stream, making the feature literally glow from within. If you want the ultimate special effect, experiment with the wonderful world of fiber optics, those glowing strands that can hang like mare's tails down a watercourse.

Right *When lighting is combined sensitively with water the results can be magical. Here the white light source is placed below the water level, picking out the edge of the stepping stone in sharp relief and contrasting with the darker foreground paving. There is just enough ambient illumination to light the blooms, which seem to float against the near-black background.*

care & maintenance

Maintenance should be preventative and not just curative. Checking features and their surrounds regularly and doing small repairs where necessary is more sensible than performing major reconstruction work after something has gone drastically wrong. In my own garden, maintenance has become part of an almost unconscious daily or weekly routine. I regularly check watercourses for leaks, clean pump filters and make sure cables, sockets and other electrical equipment are in good condition. The mortar in brickwork or stonework of raised pools or other features may need replacing from time to time. It will also be particularly important to check the coping around pools. Unsound coping could result in a nasty accident or even the drowning of an unsuspecting child.

It is a good idea to install a leaf net in autumn, particularly if there are nearby trees. This can be left in place for a month or so and then removed, the contents being ideal for the compost heap. If leaves are not removed from the water's surface, or prevented from settling there in the first place, they can lead to

Above right *Reflections are the crowning glory of still or gently rippling water, but to achieve this degree of clarity a perfect ecological balance, or a sophisticated filtration system, must be in place. The former is preferable.*

Right *Leaves in this situation form a richly patterned aquatic carpet that is frankly gorgeous. However, you should be aware that a substantial buildup of leaves can lead to the release of methane gas. This might be dangerous for fish if the pond freezes over. A leaf net could be the answer.*

Opposite *A beautifully planted pool. Remember, however, that many of these plants are rampant growers and need thinning on an annual basis, to the benefit of your slower-growing friends, of course!*

blockages in the pump, which can in turn lead to costly repairs.

In my pools I have two relatively large pumps and both have performed perfectly for six years. Sooner or

Rich planting turns a man-made pool into a feature that complements the surroundings and looks natural. A pool this size is big enough to contain its own ecosystem, which will take care of a lot of the maintenance on its own. A helping hand will be needed once in a while, though. Most of the plants here will need thinning out at least once a year in order to prevent the pool from becoming completely overrun with planting.

later one will fail and so I have a brand new one in reserve that can quickly be installed to minimize disruption. In warm weather, waterfalls can provide fish with invaluable oxygen, so it can be dangerous to the fish when a pump breaks and leaves the water still.

Occasionally pool liners can split—or acquire holes—one very good reason for encasing them in concrete. Should an exposed liner be punctured by a fork or a misdirected dart, it can be patched. Remember to leave the offending object in place so that you can find the hole easily. The closer it is to the surface the easier the job will be, since the pool or watercourse will need to be drained down to that point and then cleaned off and dried. Patch kits can be bought from a water garden specialist; a square of new liner should be stuck over the hole and allowed to dry completely before refilling.

Maintenance should be preventative and not just curative.

Right *There are moments of creation that need no description. Look, feel and understand.*

planting

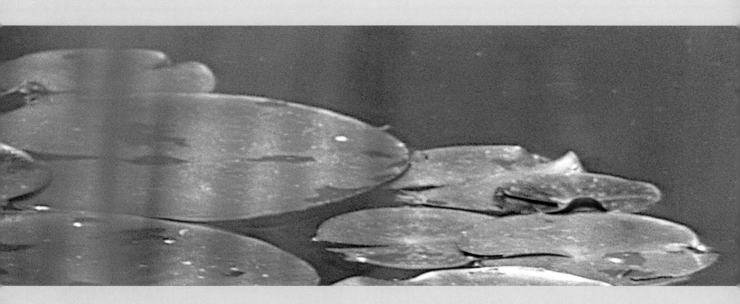

Plants will bring your water feature to life, softening the edges of a pool or rill, introducing color and interest throughout the year and blending everything into the wider garden landscape. Planting in water is easy as long as you understand a few basic techniques—and believe me, the effort is more than worthwhile.

planting

Any area of water needs to have a balanced ecosystem encompassing plants, fish and a whole range of insects and other life forms. Together, these will ensure a healthy environment, but without them, even with complicated pumps, filters and incidental equipment, it will be almost impossible to prevent problems such as algae. The balance of a pond depends on a number of things, the most simple of which are sunlight, minerals, oxygen and carbon dioxide. A pool without plants allows algae to use the sun's energy, together with the minerals, which in turn make the water green. Algae can grow incredibly quickly. In a short time they choke your pool and prevent you from being able to see the fish and other inhabitants.

A well-stocked pond uses submerged species that feed on the minerals, marginal plants that grow with their toes in the water and other plants, such as lilies, that have floating leaves. By shading approximately half the pond's surface, the lily pads reduce the available sunlight and the energy that it provides for algae.

Right *Planting in a pool can be as simple or as complicated as you want it to be. It would be difficult to improve on the classical beauty of lilies.*
Opposite *A richer ecological habitat is achieved with a richer mix of planting, including ferns and calla lilies.*

Above *There is always a wonderful visual dialogue between horizontal water and vertical foliage. Horizontal foliage floats on the surface of the water, as do these great lily pads with their shining flowers, whereas vertical foliage stands upright from, or falls down into, the pool, flowing with the movement of the water.*

Most plants for water features can be obtained from good water garden centers along with any equipment you may require. All plants, apart from a few that actually float on the surface of the water, need to be planted. You can buy perforated planting baskets to do this, but it is an excellent idea to think ahead, if possible, and build in planting beds while you are actually constructing the pond. These beds can be incorporated around the edge of the pool area, just below the water line for marginal plants, and in deep water for plants with floating leaves. If you are using a liner, you can build the beds on top of it, but remember that you will need a simple foundation underneath to carry the weight. If the beds are brickwork, the foundation should be twice as wide as the walls. The depth of the foundation depends on the type of soil, but it should be at least 9 inches deep.

Plants provide stability for both the banks and the eye, creating points of interest along the way.

Aquatic plants should be grown in good-quality top soil, which can be used to fill both built-in beds and movable planting baskets. You should line the baskets with burlap to prevent the soil from washing out of them; top the soil with a layer of gravel for the same reason. My own pools are pretty big and I have used large plastic crates as planters for lilies and cut-down plastic garbage cans for my marginals, both of which allow ample room for development. Plants are not particularly fussy about what type of container they grow in—just make sure the container is black, which will make it less visible.

Although you can plant during most of the summer, late spring is best, when growth is vigorous and the water is starting to warm up. Aquatics need very little

Above *Streams are full of movement, swirling and ever changing. Plants provide stability for both the banks and the eye, creating points of interest along the way. These monkey flowers will thrive in such conditions.*

attention beyond thinning out. This can be quite drastic for very vigorous species. I have a big sorting-out session each spring. This involves cutting back and removing plants from their containers to divide them. It can be hard work moving the big containers, and two people make the job much easier. In a thriving water system like mine, a second, slightly less drastic, session is needed in late summer, in order to thin things out again and open up all the right sight lines.

We have already discussed bog gardens, with their ideal growing conditions for all those wonderful damp-loving, large-leafed species, as well as the delightful primroses, marsh marigolds and iris. Very often, however, your pool will be set in the midst of a garden that has far drier conditions. There are many plants that will grow in either wet or dry areas, including iris, bamboo, grasses, hostas, purple loosestrife, lysimachia and fairy wand. With a little irrigation you can extend the range considerably. If you have room, think about incorporating the wonderful and giant *Gunnera manicata* and the slightly less vigorous *Rheum palmatum*.

As far as maintenance is concerned, there should be very little needed if everything is balanced correctly. There is a lot of nonsense going around about draining pools and cleaning them out—to do so would simply destroy the ecosystem and most of the insect life. Obviously, if an old pool is completely silted up it does need attention, but my pools are now six years old and nowhere near a clear-out. In other words, let sleeping dogs, or pools, lie.

There is always a wonderful visual dialogue between horizontal water and vertical foliage. Horizontal foliage floats on the surface of the water, whereas vertical foliage stands upright from, or falls down into, the pool, flowing with the movement of the water.

Above *Astilbes are one of the best waterside or bog garden plants. Once the blooms have finished I leave the brown seed heads on throughout the winter, since they look so attractive. Flower colors include red, pink and white.*

fish

& wildlife

I'm something of a child when it comes to ponds. I love to watch the creatures that live in the water. There are fish darting about, dragonflies hatching and bees coming to drink. The wonderful thing is that most of this just happens without our interference. Get the basics right and the rest follows naturally.

fish & wildlife

Plants combine with fish, insects and all kinds of other creatures to build up a complete and low-maintenance ecosystem. This in turn attracts birds, toads and frogs, which will live off the aquatic environment you have created. You can be serious or laid-back about all this and I have to admit that I fall into the latter category. Equally, I have to say that it all works like a dream.

The secret is to have lots of space, and I do have plenty of water, both still and moving. A custom-built stream links upper and lower pools and this, now that the planting has developed, works as a natural filter, keeping the whole system crystal clear. My fish came as fairground prizes, and from the original half dozen or so, we now have more than I can count, and big ones too. They are all common goldfish but they have interbred,

producing all kinds of colors and fin formations. The pools have ample planting and corners that are secluded enough to encourage breeding. The environment is so rich that I never have to feed the fish. Damselflies and dragonflies abound with their magical colors, water beetles and water boatmen skate and slide, while frogs hop out at you at the most unexpected moments. The stream's beaches allow the frogs to get out and also encourage small mammals to come and drink. The abundant water snails, which must have come in on the plants, have proved invaluable in helping to filter the water.

All I did was introduce plants and fish; the rest just happened, as it will for you too. Many people complain about mosquitoes around water, and it's true, we do

Left *Attracting visitors such as toads to a water feature plays a vital role in creating and maintaining a healthy and balanced ecosystem.*
Opposite *A pool in the prime of life with fish, plants and all kinds of other wildlife thriving in abundance. Just watch out for herons; if necessary stretch a single strand of wire 6 inches above the ground right around the pool as a deterrent.*

have a few, but more end up being eaten by swallows and frogs than feeding on us!

If you are a fish fancier, koi carp may be your specialty. These fish can live quite happily in a natural pool, but some people want perfectly clear water without too much vegetation to get in the way of their expensive pets. In this case you need to install filtration systems. Although effective, these do seem to produce a sterile-looking result. It can be useful to have a number of bottom feeders, such as tench, which also help to keep the pool clean.

It is very important to remember to keep water clear in freezing conditions, in order to prevent a buildup of lethal gasses. Never break the ice, as the shock waves can stun fish. You can buy small floating immersion heaters, which are both economic to run and do the job perfectly.

Above left *This kind of habitat is superb around a pool with damp conditions, ample leaf litter and shallow beaches. Don't be overzealous with maintenance or you could so easily upset this balance!*
Left *Apart from the visual beauty of these stems, they will provide the perfect hatching place for dragonfly larvae. Watch the newly emerged fly dry his wings and depart in all his glory.*

Right *What a fine fellow—and one of your most trusted garden friends. He will eat vast quantities of unwelcome guests. Live in harmony with your pond life and they will pay you back a thousandfold.*

address book

Landscapedirect.com
Tel: (800) 397-5742
Fax: (502) 326-9791 or
(310) 362-8665
E-mail: info@landscapedirect.com
Web site:
www.landscapedirect.com

Landscaping and gardening products sold on-line

PONDFiltration, Inc.
11551 Rupp Drive
Burnsville, MN 55337
Tel: (888) 766-3051 or
(800) 882-5327 for local dealer
or catalog
Fax: (612) 890-0459
E-mail: nomoregreenwater@
pondfiltration.com
Web site: www.pondfiltration.com

Pond filters, pumps and supplies

Pond Supplies of America
1204 Deer Street
Yorkville, IL 60560
Tel: (888) 742-5772 for local
dealer or catalog
Fax: (630) 553-9618
E-mail: pondsuppli@aol.com
Web site: www.pondsupplies.com

Pond kits, filters and supplies

Resource Conservation Technology, Inc.
2633 North Calvert Street
Baltimore, MD 21218
Tel: (800) 477-7724 for catalog
Fax: (410) 366-1202
Web site:
www.pondtechnology.com

Supplies and equipment for ponds over 250 gallons

American Horticultural Society
7931 East Boulevard Drive
Alexandria, VA 22308
Tel: (703) 768-5700
Fax: (703) 768-8700
Web site: www.ahs.org

American Society of Landscape Architects
636 Eye Street, NW
Washington, D.C. 20001-3736
Tel: (202) 898-2444
Fax: (202) 898-1155
E-mail: scahill@asla.org
Web site: www.asla.org

Associated Koi Clubs of America
P.O. Box 1
Midway City, CA 92655
Tel: (800) 646-1685
E-mail: debbyt@koiusa.com
Web site: www.koiusa.com

Garden Club of America
14 East 60th Street
New York, NY 10022
Tel: (212) 753-8287
Fax: (212) 753-0134
E-mail: info@gcamerica.org
Web site: www.gcamerica.org

National Gardening Association
180 Flynn Avenue
Burlington, VT 05401
Tel: (802) 863-1308
Fax: (802) 863-5962
Web site: www.garden.org

Equipment, Liners, Preformed Pools, Pumps, etc.

Anne Hathaway
2101 Tula at Bennet Street
Atlanta, GA 30309
Tel: (404) 352-4153
Fax: (770) 421-0821
E-mail: sales@millstones.com
Web site: www.millstones.com

Antique, historic millstones collected from all over the South

Aqua Art Pond Specialists
11G Poco Way, Suite 154
American Canyon, CA 94589
Tel: (800) 997-9164 or
(707) 642-7663 for catalog
Fax: (707) 642-7119
E-mail: aquaart@napanet.net
Web site: www.aquaart.com

Pond and water garden equipment; mail-order only

Both Sides of the Door
2205 Union Street
Oakland, CA 94607
Tel: (510) 663-5600
E-mail: bothside@pacbell.net
Web site:
www.bothsidesofthedoor.com

Designer of ponds, waterfalls and water gardens

Broadmoor Landscape Supply
1350 El Camino Real
South San Francisco, CA 94080
Tel: (650) 761-1515
Fax: (650) 761-1520
Web site:
www.broadmoorlumber.com

Ponds, waterfalls, fountains, statuary, water garden supplies, fish and aquatic plants

Home Depot
2455 Paces Ferry Road
(corporate office)
Atlanta, GA 30339
Tel: (800) 430-3376 or
(770) 433-8211 for store locations
Web site: www.homedepot.com

Home improvement supplies, including pumps, preformed ponds and liners

Paved Areas

Genest Concrete Works, Inc.
P.O. Box 151
Wilson Street
Sanford, ME 04073
Tel: (207) 324-3250
Fax: (207) 490-5076
E-mail:
sales@genest-concrete.com
Web site:
www.genest-concrete.com

Precast interlocking concrete and brick pavers, architectural blocks and masonry supplies

Hanover Architectural Products
240 Bender Road
Hanover, PA 17331
Tel: (800) 426-4242
Fax: (717) 637-7145
E-mail: hanpaver@sun-link.com
Web site:
www.hanoverpavers.com

Precast concrete and reconstructed stone paving

Rhodes Masonry, Inc.
2011 East Olive Street
Seattle, WA 98122
Tel: (206) 726-0437
Fax: (206) 709-3004 or 709-3003
E-mail: info@rhodesmasonry.com
Web site:
www.rhodesmasonry.com

Precast paving, architectural stone and brick

Natural Stone Paving and Rock

ASN Natural Stone
200 Kansas Street, Suite 209
San Francisco, CA 94103
Tel: (415) 626-2616 or
(800) 827-8663
Fax: (415) 626-3578
E-mail: asnstone@pacbell.net
Web site: www.asnstone.com

Imported natural stone for indoor and outdoor uses

Dixie Cut Stone & Marble
6128 Dixie Highway
Bridgeport, MI 48722
Tel: (800) 968-8282
Fax: (517) 777-9700
E-mail: limestone@dixiestone.com
Web site: www.dixiestone.com

Architectural landscaping stone, limestone, marble and other natural stones

Decking

Mendocino Specialty Lumber Company
P.O. Box 519
Hydesville, CA 95547
Tel: (707) 726-0339
Fax: (707) 726-0319
E-mail: wood@oldgrowth.com
Web site: www.oldgrowth.com

Reclaimed wood from old-growth redwood trees harvested before 1930

Features/Sculpture

Elegant Accents West Inc.
604 McClary Avenue
Oakland, CA 94621
Tel: (510) 568-6255 for catalog
Fax: (510) 568-6360
E-mail: elegant@pacbell.net
Web site:
www.gardendiscovery.com

Japanese garden ornaments, fountains and sculptures

Maine Millstones
P.O. Box 228
Southport, ME 04576
Tel: (207) 633-6091
Fax: (207) 633-6095

Genuine, custom-made millstones

Florentine Craftsmen, Inc.
46-24 28th Street
Long Island City, NY 11101
Tel: (718) 937-7632 for catalog
Fax: (718) 937-9858
E-mail:
info@florentinecraftsmen.com
Web site:
www.florentinecraftsmen.com

Fountains, urns, statuary, furniture and garden ornaments

Proler Oeggerli
2611 Worthington Street
Dallas, TX 75204
Tel: (214) 871-2233
Fax: (214) 871-0101
E-mail:
gardenantiks@earthlink.net

Antique fountains, urns and statuary

Stone Forest
213 Saint Francis Drive
Santa Fe, NM 87501
Tel: (888) 682-2987 or
(505) 986-8883 for catalog
Fax: (505) 982-2712
E-mail: sfi@stoneforest.com
Web site: www.stoneforest.com

Hand-carved granite fountains, stone sinks, birdbaths, spheres and lanterns

Plants and Aquatic Nurseries

Lilypons Water Gardens
Tel: (800) 723-7667 or
(800) 999-LILY for catalog and locations in Maryland and Texas
Fax: (800) 879-5459
E-mail: info@lilypons.com
Web site: www.lilypons.com

Aquatic plants, fish and water gardening supplies

Paradise Water Gardens
14 May Street
Whitman, MA 02382
Tel: (800) 955-0161 for catalog
Fax: (800) 966-4591
E-mail: pstetson@
paradisewatergardens.com
Web site:
www.paradisewatergardens.com

Aquatic plants, fish, fountains, pools and pumps

The Water Garden
5594 Dayton Boulevard
Chattanooga, TN 37415
Tel: (423) 870-2838
Fax: (423) 870-3382
E-mail: info@watergarden.com
Web site: www.watergarden.com

Aquatic plants, fish, ponds, pumps and a wide range of water garden supplies

Koi Carp Specialists

Koi Unlimited Water Garden Center
5305-A Jefferson Pike
Frederick, MD 21703/
Tel: (301) 473-5518
Web site: www.koi-unlimited.com

Koi and goldfish, fish supplies, aquatic and bog plants and pond equipment

Utah Koi and Fancy Goldfish Farm
3494 West 6925 South
West Jordan, UT 84084-1727
Tel: (801) 966-4318
E-mail: utahkoi@worldnet.att.net
Web site: home.att.net/~utahkoi/

Koi and goldfish, fish supplies

index

Page numbers in *italics* refer to illustrations.

A
acrylic *38*, 44, 50
algae 80
aquatic centers 56, 70, 83
aquatic planting 14, 66, 83–4
architectural effects 12, *37*, 55, 63
astilbes 52, *53*, *85*
asymmetrical style 24, *24–5*

B
baskets 42, *61*, *69*, 83
beaches *36*, 88
    construction *58*
birds 28, 88, 90
bog gardens 28, 33, 52, *52–3*, 68, *68–9*, 84
boulders 12, *26*, *27*, 28, *47*, 48, 66
bowls 16, *30*, *40*, 42, 48, 66
budgeting 14

C
canals 34–7, *34–7*
care 30, 44, 74–6
children 28, 48, 74

choosing a style 20–7
classical water features 42, 44, *44*
cobblestones *20*, *25*, 28, *31*, *36*, 46, 48, *63*
concrete 8, 62, *67*, 76, 68
construction 14, 54, 55
    beaches *58*
    fountains *63*, *64*, 65
    pools *56*, *58*, *61*, *62*, *69*
    waterfalls *59*, 70
coping 33, *57*, 60, *63*, 74
copper features 43, 44, *70–1*
costs 14

D
dadaism *21*
decking *19*, *24*, *25*, 26, 33

E
ecosystem 30, 60, 80, 84, 88
electricity 66, 72, 74
equipment 12, 70, 80

F
fashion 8, 20
filters 74, 80, 88, 90
fish 6, 28, 30, 38, 60, 76, 80, 87, 88–90, *91*

floating balls 8, 40
flow adjustment 48, 70
focal points 16, 33, 38, *48*
foliage 39, *50*, *52*, 72, *82*
formal style 8, 12, *19*, 22, *22–3*, *31*, 34, *34*
fountains 34, 38–40, *38–41*, 70
    bubble fountains *33*, 38, 66
    construction *63*, *64*, 65
frogs 88, 90, *91*

G
garden buildings 24, 33
garden centers 12, 42, 56, 66, 83
garden design 11, 12, 20, 44
garden rooms 22, *37*, 44
glass beads 48, *65*
Gunnera manicata 52, *52*, 84

H
habitat 6, 28, 30, 60, 80, 84, 88
hedges 20, 22, 33
historical influences 6, *14*, 34, 40
horizontals *8*, *26*, 34, *82*

hostas *46*, 52, 84
house/garden link 6–8, *17*, *18*, *19*, 20, 24, 30, 34
humor 16, *28*

I
informal style 12, 26, *26–7*
insects 30, 80, 84, 87, 88
inspiration 12, 28
iris 52, *53*, 84

L
leaf nets 74–6
leaks 60, 62, 74, 76
lighting 50, 72, *73*
lilies 34, *67*, 80, *80*, *81*, *82*
liners *56–9*, *56–60*, 66, 68, 76
    repairing 76
Lutyens, Sir Edwin 34

M
maintenance 30, 44, 74–6
masks 16, 42–4
Mediterranean garden *51*
mesh *64*, *65*, 66
millstones 8, 46, 66
modern movement 24, *67*
mood boards 12

mosquitoes 30, 88–90
movement 6, *9*, *20*, *36*, 37,
 50, *83*

N
natural effects 26, *37*, 55
 natural features,
 studying 12, 37

O
oxygenation 14, 38, 76, 80

P
paths 22
paving 14, *19*, 24, 33, *35*, *63*
piers *65*, 66
pipes 44, 46, 48, 70
planting *26*, 28, 42, 50
 aquatic 14, 66, 83–4
 planting beds 83
plants 6, 12, 28, 30, 78, *32*,
 34, 52, *53*, 60, 80, *81*, 84
pools 11, 12, 16, 28, *30–3*,
 30–3, 56, 68, 78
 construction 56, *58*, *61*,
 62, *69*
 draining 76, 84
 pre-formed pools 60, *61*
primroses 52, *53*, 84
pumps 14, 38, 44, 46–8, 64–6,
 70, *70–1*, 74–6, 80
purple loosestrife *53*, 84
pyramids *37*, *40*

R
reflections 6, *15*, 16, *20*, *21*,
 33, *33*, 40, 50, *65*, 74
reservoirs 44, 46–8, 64–6
Rheum palmatum 52, 84
rills 12, *19*, 22, 28, *31*, 34–7,
 34–7, 56, 78
rock 12, 14, *26*, *27*, 37, *37*

S
safety 28, 48, 72, 74
slides 12, *29*, 48
small-scale features *14*, 16,
 30, 42, 46–8, *46–9*, 64–6,
 64–6, 70–1
sound 6, 16, 38, 44, 50
spheres 8, 40
spouts 16, *42*
stainless steel 40, 48, *65*
streams 34–7, *34–7*, 56, 60,
 68, 88
structural features 50, *50–1*
styles 20–7

T
tanks *64*, *65*, 64–6
taps *45*
terraces 14, 22, 24, 33
thinning out 83–4
toads 88, *88*
trees 12, 14, *18*, *23*, 24, 74

V
verticals *8*, *18*, *26*, 34, *37*, 82
views 16, *19*, 22, 33

W
walls 14
 wall-mounted features
 42–4, *42–5*
water curtains *51*
water ports 28, *29*, 50
water stairs 22, 50
waterfalls *27*, 56, 60, 70, 76
 construction *59*, *70*
wildlife 6, 14, 28, 88–90

First published in 2000 by Conran Octopus Limited
a part of Octopus Publishing Group
2-4 Heron Quays London E14 4JP

www.conran-octopus.co.uk

SOMA Books is an imprint of Bay Books & Tapes,
555 De Haro St., No. 220, San Francisco, CA 94107.

For the Conran Octopus edition:
Commissioning Editor: Stuart Cooper
Senior Editor: Helen Woodhall
Copy Editor: Helena Attlee
Editorial Assistant: Alexandra Kent
Creative Director: Leslie Harrington
Designer: Lucy Gowans
Picture Researcher: Mel Watson
Production Controller: Suzanne Sharpless

For the SOMA edition:
Copy Editor: Karen O'Donnell Stein
Proofreader: Ken DellaPenta
Production: Jeff Brandenburg

Library of Congress Cataloging-in-Publication Data

Stevens, David, 1943-
   SOMA Basics—Water features/ David Stevens
      —North American ed.
   p.cm.—(SOMA Basics)
   Rev. ed. of: Conran Octopus contemporary water
   features. 2000.
   ISBN 1-57959-062-4 (pbk.)
      1. Water gardens. I. Title: Water Features. II.
   Stevens, David, 1943–Conran Octopus
   contemporary water features. III. Title. IV. Series.

   SB423 .S684 2001
   635.9'674—dc21   00-027992

Printed in China

10 9 8 7 6 5 4 3 2 1

Distributed by Publishers Group West

Author's acknowledgments

A finished book is only the tip of an iceberg of planning and hard work involving far more people than just the author! Special thanks to my editor, Helen Woodhall and my secretary, Angela Bambridge.

Publisher's acknowledgments

The publisher would like to thank the following photographers and agencies for their kind permission to reproduce the photographs in this book:
2 Jerry Harpur/Designer: Jean-Pierre Delettre, Chaumont-sur-Loire, France,1998; 4–5 Tamarra Richards/The Garden Picture Library; 7 Deborah Davis/Photonica; 8 *left* Lanny Provo; 8 *right* Bart van Leuven/Landscape Architects: Wilfried Buls & Paul Claes, Belgium; 9 K. Hashimoto/Photonica; 10–11 Andrew Lawson/Hampton Court Flower Show 1999/Designer: Karen Maskell; 13 Christi Carter/ The Garden Picture Library/ Designer: Kent Gullickson, CA, USA; 14 *above* Steven Wooster/ Designer: Anthony Paul; 14 *below* Clive Nichols/Chelsea Flower Show 1997/Designer:Roger Platts; 15 Simon Kenny/Belle Magazine/Architect: Mike Macaulay, Australia; 16 Liz Eddison; 17 Gil Hanly/ Owner: Dr. M Pohl, Auckland, New Zealand; 18 Earl Carter/Belle Magazine/ Metropolis Urban Space Design, Melbourne, Australia; 19 *above* Bart van Leuven/ Landscape Architect:Claes en Humblet Tuinarchitecten NV, Belgium; 19 *below* Ian Pleeth/Acres Wild Garden Design; 20 John Glover/ Hampton Court Flower Show 1995/ Designer:Naila Green; 21 Leigh Clapp/Living Exteriors Garden Design, Australia; 22 *left* Liz Eddison/Chelsea Flower Show 1999/Christie's Fine Art Auctioneers/ Designer: George Carter; 22 *right* Jerry Harpur/Hazleby House, Berkshire; 23 Leigh Clapp/ Designer: Swinburne TAFE, Australia; 24 *left* Marijke Heuff/Mien Ruys, Holland; 24 *above right* Malcolm Birkett/Designer: John Brookes/Kings Heath Park, Birmingham; 24 *below right* Bart van Leuven/ Landscape Architect: Jean Noel Capart; 25 N et P Mioulane/Mise au Point/Designer: Christophe Caixtois; 26 *left* Gary Rogers/ The Garden Picture Library; 26 *above right* Ian Smith/ Acres Wild Garden Design; 26 *below right* Gil Hanly/ Garden Design by Isabelle Greene and Associates, FASLA, Santa Barbara Landscape Architect; 27 Roger Foley/Designers: Oehme, van Sweden & Associates; 28 Marijke Heuff/Artist: Tamas Asszonyi; 29 Marianne Majerus/Hampton Court Flower Show 1999 /Designer:David Stevens; 30 John Glover; 31 Brigitte Thomas/The Garden Picture Library/ Designer: J. Wirtz, Belgium; 32 Brigitte Perdereau/ Plantbessin Garden, France; 33 Ian Smith/ Acres Wild Garden Design; 34 Gary Rogers; 35 Undine Prohl; 36 John Glover/Hampton Court Flower Show 1992; 37 *left* Roger Foley/ Designer: Sam Williamson and Associates, USA; 37 *right* Marianne Majerus/Designer: Marc Schollen; 38 John Glover/Hampton Court Flower Show 1994/ Horticultural Therapy; 39 Elizabeth Whiting & Associates; 40 *left* John Glover/National Rose Society Garden/ Sculptor: William Pye; 40 *right* Jerry Harpur/Designer: Brent Collins & Associates, Hong Kong; 41 John Glover/Chelsea Flower Show 1995/Designer Fiona Lawrenson; 42 Andrew Lawson; 43 Justyn Willsmore/Hampton Court Flower Show 1997/Chenies Aquatics; 44 J S Sira/ The Garden Picture Library/Chelsea Flower Show 1994/ Haddonstone Ltd; 45 Bart van Leuven/ Landscape Architects: Wilfried Buls & Paul Claes, Belgium; 46 John Glover/Designer: Alan Titchmarsh; 47 Gary Rogers; 48 Mark Bolton; 49 Leigh Clapp/ Mistilis Garden, Australia; 50 Malcolm Birkett/Chelsea Flower Show 1999/ Marie Curie Cancer Care Garden/Designer: Patrick McCann; 51 Andrew Lawson/ Chelsea Flower Show 1998/ Designer: David Stevens; 52 Marianne Majerus, Bushy Park; 53 *above* Andrew Lawson/Marwood Hill, Devon; 53 *below* Marianne Majerus/ Fairhaven Garden Trust, Norfolk; 54–55 John Glover; 57 Brigitte Thomas/ The Garden Picture Library; 58 Liz Eddison; 59 Liz Eddison/ Designers: Bunny Guinness and Peter Eustance, Chelsea Flower Show 1999, Wyevale Garden Centres; 61 John Glover; 62 Michael Paul/ The Garden Picture Library/Designer: Anthony Paul; 63 Andrew Lawson/Designer: Paul Bangay, Australia; 64 Clive Nichols; 65 Andrew Lawson/ Hampton Court Flower Show 1999/ Designer: David Stevens; 67 Lanny Provo; 68 Andrew Lawson/ Marwood Hill, Devon; 71 Derek St Romaine/ Hampton Court Flower Show 1994/Age Concern/ Designer: Barbara Hunt; 73 Marianne Majerus; 74 *above* Trevor Mein/Belle Magazine/ Landscape Design: Andrew McFarland, Australia; 74 *below* S & O Mathews; 75 Ron Sutherland/ The Garden Picture Library/Eco Design, Australia; 76 Brigitte Perdereau/ Chaumont-sur-Loire, France; 77 Andrew Lawson/ Designer: Tom Sitta, Australia; 78–79 Roger Foley; 80 Ursel Borstell; 81 Ron Sutherland/ The Garden Picture Library/ Designer: Anthony Paul; 82 Roger Foley/Designers: Oehme, van Sweden & Associates; 83 Sunniva Harte/ The Garden Picture Library; 85 S & O Mathews/ Cobblers, Sussex; 86–87 Justyn Willsmore/ RHS Wisley, Surrey; 88 David Bevan; 89 Justyn Willsmore/ RHS Wisley, Surrey; 90 *above* Angela Hampton/ Ecoscene; 90 *below* J C Mayer – G Le Scanff/The Garden Picture Library/Jardin de Talos, France; 91 Paul Stevens/Planet Earth Pictures.

We apologize in advance for any unintentional omission and would be pleased to insert the appropriate acknowledgment in any subsequent edition.